Tinka Elephant's Nose

Written and Illustrated
by
Sue Camm

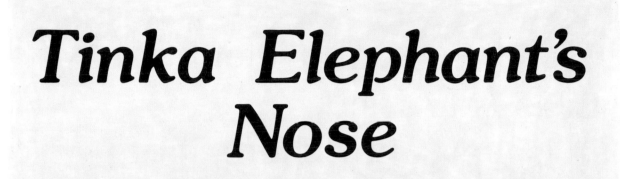

GONDOLA

Tinka the baby elephant
lives in Africa.
It is very hot there, but
Tinka's home is in a cool
and shady forest.
Tinka has a very long nose.
It is called a trunk.
All elephants have trunks.
Tinka likes to play
in the forest.

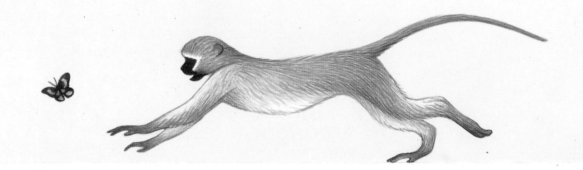

Mick Monkey makes fun
of Tinka Elephant.
"You do look funny!
My nose is neat and flat,
so I do not bump it when
I climb the trees," he says.
Mick jumps onto a branch
and swings by his tail.
"Maybe my nose is too
long," says Tinka.

Poll Parrot makes fun
of Tinka Elephant.
"You do look funny! I have
a hard beak. I can crack
nuts open with my beak,"
says Poll Parrot.
Then, Poll spreads her
wings and flies away.
"I am sure my nose is too
long," says Tinka.

Little Wild Pig makes fun of Tinka Elephant.
"You do look funny! My nose is short and strong. I can dig up nice roots to eat. Look, like this."
He digs with his nose in the soft ground.
"Now I know my nose is too long!" says Tinka.

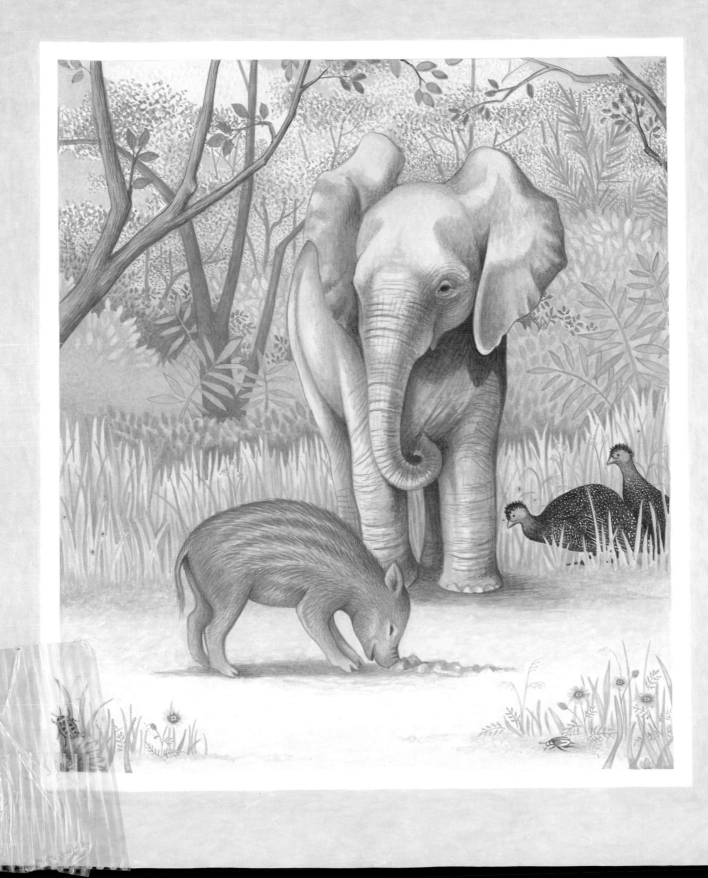

Tiny Giraffe makes fun
of Tinka Elephant.
"You do look funny! I have
a short black nose. Your
nose is so long it must
get in the way when you
run!" says Tiny Giraffe.
Then, he flicks his tail
and runs into the forest.
"I wish I had a short nose
like Tiny," says
Tinka Elephant.

"The animals make fun of my long nose," says Tinka to her mother. "Can I make my trunk grow short?"
"You are silly," says her mother. "A long nose is a great help to an elephant. Just wait and see!
Now go and play so I can have a sleep."

Tinka plays by the river.
Mick Monkey is on the
other side of the river.
"How can I cross over?" he
says. "I cannot swim!"
"Wait, I can help you,"
says Tinka.
See how she helps Mick to
cross the river.
"I am sorry I made fun of
your nose. It is
a great help!"

Who is this in the river?
Splash! Splash!
"Help!" says Poll Parrot.
"Get me out of the water!"
See how Tinka pulls her out.
"Thank you," says Poll.
"I fell in when I was
washing my tail. Your trunk
has saved me. I am glad
that you have a long nose!"

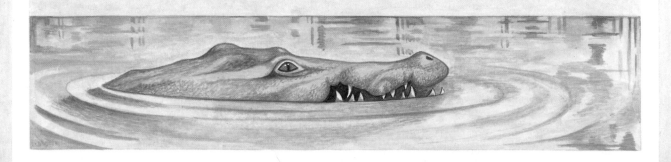

Tinka and her new friends
meet Little Wild Pig as
he digs up some roots.
"The best root goes under
this heavy log. I cannot
dig it up," he says.
Tinka can help. See how
she moves the heavy log.
"I will not make fun of
your nose again," says
Little Wild Pig
as he runs away.

Tiny Giraffe needs help.
"I like to eat new green
leaves. The best ones are
at the top of the tree.
But I am not big yet and
I cannot get them."
"I can get them for you,"
says Tinka. See how she
picks the new green leaves.
"A long nose can be a
great help after
all!" says Tinka.

Tinka sniffs the air.
"What a funny smell!"
she says.
Poll Parrot can see a long
way. "Smoke!" she says.
"There is a fire in the forest.
What can we do?"
Tinka knows what to do.
She puts her trunk in the
air. She calls to all the
elephants in
the forest.

Mother Elephant and all
the big elephants come
to help.
"We must get water to put
out the fire!" says Tinka.
The elephants go to the
river and they suck lots
of water into their trunks.
See how they put out
the fire.

The fire is out and the
forest is safe again.
"Hurray!" say Mick Monkey
and Poll Parrot.
"Hurray!" say Little Wild
Pig and Tiny Giraffe.
"Three cheers for all the
elephants!" they say.
"Three cheers for Tinka
the Elephant's nose!"

Say these words again

elephant	giraffe
monkey	parrot
shady	flicks
climb	swings
branch	crack
leaves	hurray
cheers	splash
spreads	heavy
friends	washing
other	mother